SAMI

SAME-SEXY MARRIAGE

A NOVELLA IN POEMS

JULIE MARIE WADE

BODY LANGUAGE

A MIDSUMMER NIGHT'S PRESS

New York

For Angie Griffin—
then as now, there as anywhere

A Midsummer Night's Press
3 Norden Drive
Glen Head NY 11545
amidsummernightspress@gmail.com
www.amidsummernightspress.com

Cover image by

Designed by Nieves Guerra.
ISBN-13: 978-1-938334-33-7
First edition.

Printed in Spain

CONTENTS

Look at it this way, I'm in love too.
Anything less would be a waste of time.

—Tom Crawford

THE SURGEON IN NEW ENGLAND

Surely he had a name, though I never learned it.
Did my mother call him Clark or Kent?
He must have had a set of biceps like Superman,
those WASP-ish good looks, and a paycheck
that would put a journalist's to shame.

But what's with the cape, the boots, the snug
bodysuit and red briefs worn on the outside?
A picture takes shape, sinks deep into the crevice
between my mother's eyes. *Distasteful*, she must
have sighed.

Despite Clark Kent's respectable, heterosexual
spectacles, was Superman possibly a little bit gay?

In the end, I bet she settled for my brother's name,
the one meant to balance our childhoods so I
wouldn't have to turn part-boy. Why shouldn't
her should-have-been son transform into a should-
have-been son-in-law right there inside the phone
booth of her mind?

Jeffrey Hamilton—it sounded good—the M.D.
perched upon his shoulder like a lucky bird.

If I married him, Reader—this surgeon,
this Jeffrey Hamilton—I must have loved him.
And my mother says, to anyone who will listen,
that I married him.

She is quick to explain how the ceremony
was small, elegant, and private—topiaries
were involved!—just family and close
friends at a Lutheran church with Lancelot's
sword for a steeple; a reception following
at the local yacht club, where the Hamiltons
have been members for years.

When was this?   June, of course!
And where again?   New England—
where my mother has never been.

Surely some suspicious friend will work up
the nerve to ask: *But isn't New England
really six separate states? Where exactly
do Jeffrey and Julie live?*

My mother would like the idea of Maine,
like Main Street and mainstream American
values and *Murder, She Wrote*. But her friends

might get to pestering about specifics, and
what would she say then? No internet at home
for a quick Google search. (Computers have
always been synonymous with sin.)
No way to confirm if Cabot Cove is even
a real place, and what if Augusta, the capital
she learned in junior high geography,
turned out to be a shithole?

I know my mother, better than anyone.
She picks Vermont—not for the green
rolling hills or the sharp white cheddar,
and certainly not for Ben and Jerry,
two men who opened an ice cream
shop together. (What's gayer than that,
what's more distasteful?)

But Vermont is home to a city called
Burlington, which must have been
booming to give the world my mother's
favorite store—straighter than a row of
two-by-fours—that Burlington Coat Factory.

And what kind of surgeon? people will wonder,
of the son-in-law from old-money Burlington,
Vermont, who loves billiards and slalom-racing

and the occasional glass of scotch; who has
a deep voice and a chiseled jaw; who never
developed a taste for ice cream, even as a child.

He specializes in hearts, of course, like the
(much younger) man—scandal!—who married
Mary Tyler Moore after she divorced the second
time. Oh, how the wholesome have fallen!
That cardiologist was Jewish, though. Not this one.
Not tall, Protestant, clean-shaven Jeffrey who
once modeled as a teen for JCPenney.

And how is Julie these days?
the same folks will soon inquire.

It's good to know I'm keeping busy, writing articles
from time to time for *The Burlington Gazette.*
(I have a following!) Friends may recall how I
once plucked away at an old typewriter in my
parents' basement, making crisp, singing sounds
where the Steinway keys beneath my fingers
only clacked.

Remember Heloise and her helpful hints?
Well, I'm a wealth of knowledge, too—
on growing orchids in your greenhouse

and strengthening your tennis serve without
bulking up your arms. (Ladies still look like
ladies in my town.)

The bravest among them is bound to press,
over Lipton tea and ginger snaps, between
a break in the Bingo numbers: *So, when do
you expect to be a grandma?*

I'm relieved to learn we don't have children,
but not to worry. Though my eggs are
approaching their best if used by date,
Jeff has friends in the fertility biz, friends
who promise forty is the new thirty if you
have the money to spend.

Keep your eyes peeled for a birth announcement
in a year or two—our darling fraternals,
little John (no homage to those Catholic
Kennedys—it's a family name!) and Jessica
after J.B. Fletcher.

Keep your eyes peeled for my mother,
in a year or two, late night at the Kinko's
on Delridge Way, rape whistle cinched
at her wrist. She'll be asking the only clerk

on duty if she can do something with stock
photos, two newborns centered on a card,
each wrapped in gender-appropriate pastel.

We have thousands of stock photos, Ma'am, the clerk
replies, mouth full of wires, thumbing the iPad
like digital roulette. *Can you be any more specific?*

Make them fair-haired, pink-cheeked, my mother
says. And if the eyes are open, make them blue.

THE SURGEON IN NEW ENGLAND, REVISITED

I've been gone so long the neighbors are
beginning to worry about me. First, it was
my husband's interminable residency; then
years he spent building his private practice.
They've watched my parents disappear into
the yawn of night—so many red-eye flights
depositing them in Burlington at dawn.

"You can't keep flying coast to coast,"
the neighbors warn, "not at your age.
Let your daughter visit you for a change."

My mother explains how she loves the
seasons in Vermont. People in the Pacific
Northwest have never seen such striking
contrasts. In autumn, we take them on long,
leaf-peeping weekends; in winter, it's skiing
in Stowe, where everyone knows they have
the best powder.

And then of course I was on bed rest with
that difficult pregnancy. What parents wouldn't

come to their only child's rescue? You can't
believe how quickly I got my figure back either,
already playing tennis twice a week. My mother
carries pictures of the twins in her wallet, flashes
them everywhere like a VIP pass, lets no one
inspect them at length.

The neighbors say how much they'd love to
meet Jessica and John—not to mention Jeffrey!—
but it's hard with their father's schedule lecturing
for the AMA. "He'll come to Seattle one of
these days," my mother assures them, "but right
now Julie and the kids go with him everywhere,
even overseas. He doesn't want to miss any
big moments." None of the neighbors
can blame him.

I hear my parents are going to meet us in Rome
this year for a three-generation family vacation.
Like Vermont, Rome is another place I've never been.
My real-life wife and I are talking vacations, too.
We're long overdue for a trip and need to redeem
our passport photos with a first international venture.

Maybe Italy, we say, day-dreaming Renaissance art,
Vespas cruising cobblestone roads, late-day gelatos

and gondola rides. Clearly, we have swallowed the
guidebooks whole. I can picture us there with our
slim luggage cases—matching styles, though hers is
prudent silver, mine a more flamboyant chartreuse.

Would we pass them in the terminal, I wonder,
that family of six—the parents sleek and glamorous,
the children small and glamorous, all moving languidly
as if in a perfume ad?

The grandfather beams in the background, and
the grandmother, her dictionary splayed, shouts
in almost Italian for someone to carry their bags.

HIDEAWAY

For my parents, "going to Vermont"
has become a euphemism—like "Netflix
and chill"—just not as sexy. They water
their ferns, put a hold on their mail, make
sure none of the faucets are dripping like
that one time—my mother's cheeks scorch
to recall—when the water bill soared
to high heaven.

If friends offer a ride to the airport,
they'll have to explain how my father's
many years as a traveling salesman come
with the perk of complimentary long-term
parking for life. So nice the car is always
waiting when we land!

The fact is, though my father traveled
for a living, he never parked at the airport,
which would have cost his company
a pretty penny even then.

I remember instead Friday evenings
rising through the one-way tiers, my mother

at the wheel—how we scanned each walkway
for a trench-coated man clasping a brown
suitcase and a gray garment bag. How he always
tended to blend in with that crowd.

So many men left their families on weekdays
for jobs on the road. Some, I suppose,
never came home. But my father was
faithful as a 1950s cocktail hour, conservative
as Daylight Savings Time. My mother said
he was just the right combination of
Paul Drake and Perry Mason.

Tonight he floors the engine at my mother's
command, headlights sweeping the heavy
dark from the road. They sail past signs
for Sea-Tac, both economy and short-term
parking lots, then merge with a hundred
other Hondas onto Interstate 5 southbound.

She will have packed a dinner for them—
that family staple of peanut butter with pickles
on white Bunny bread, brown apple slices, and
chocolate pudding cellophaned for later
at a rest stop. He'll play his Roger Whitaker
tapes and hum along softly. She'll make a grocery
list for tomorrow in the margins of the map.

It should be noted this is not all together unpleasant. It should be noted they are not entirely bereft in my absence. And at nine o'clock sharp, in accordance with the timers, all the lamps in their homes will switch on.

MY DAUGHTER'S A LESBIAN, AND ALL I GOT IS THIS LOUSY BEACH HOUSE

Grandpa John bought a plot of land on
the Oregon Coast in 1956—when sand
was cheaper than dirt, he said.

My father took me there in the 1980s,
only once. We stood on a dune blooming
with grass, while my mother, not partial
to beaches or oceans, sat in the car
and sulked.

"This was my dad's dream," he told
me—"to bring the whole family here
for the one warm month of the year."

But Grandpa John died young, in 1971,
and my father's sister died young, too,
without ever marrying anyone.

"We'll build a house on this land," Dad
promised me, as we fidgeted in our slickers,
cinching the hoods. "When you grow up,

you can come every summer with your
husband and kids." In the distance,
my mother laid on the horn.

But when I grew up, I took a hard
pass on the husband, declined
the coverage for kids. I moved
to a condo on the other coast
with the woman I love, where
the beach is our own backyard.

My father sends letters to Florida
now, sometimes frantic, other times
stern. "It's your duty to return
to Washington," he writes—then
clarifies that I must come alone.

"We built the beach house," he revealed
 in a recent note. "Your mother has
five-thousand square feet to decorate,
and she agrees with me that it's a lovely
refuge from the city."

When I send my mother a housewarming
gift—rustic lantern with votive candles
and a coffee table book—her reply belies

the daisy stationery, the sweet peas on
her forever stamp, but not the bare
left corner:

"Who in the name of all that's holy
told you about our house at the shore?
Don't get any bright ideas"—now the
peaks in her script turn sharp as spears
—"about coming here and ruining
everything I've worked so hard for."

UNDISCLOSED ADDRESS

Somewhere in Oregon my mother
stands in her new spare kitchen,
white walls glaring, impatient,
an echo built into every crook
and cupboard.

She has the spoon rack and the spice
rack and the wine rack, even the little
hammock where bananas are
supposed to recline. Paint swatches
on the counter have begun mocking—
Do you want Riesling walls or Chardonnay?
How about Champagne?

The question underneath these questions,
always: *What will the new neighbors say?*

Today she's waiting for a Sears home
delivery: a new front-load washer and
a dryer she will never use. My mother
prefers the clothesline, always has,
standing in the high-fenced yard
with her apron on, pockets bulging

with pegs and a small radio wobbling
with Frank Sinatra songs.

Once she even had a daughter to help her
with this chore. In matching aprons, pink
with all the frills, they'd shake the bed sheets
together, pin them against the wind.
Everything seemed so possible then—
the little girl who'd play piano and
photograph well, go on to win at pageants,
claim Sea-Fair Princess and Prom Queen
the same year.

Their new house has far more closet
space than the old. Already she's started
a discrete re-gifting bin. There's a book
about lighthouses that someone might like;
it's glossy at least and expensive-looking.
And there's a lantern in a style called
shabby chic. *Could these oxymorons
get any more moronic?* she sighs,
wedging it back in the box.

WHEN MY PARENTS JOIN
A SENIOR CENTER IN ------------,
OREGON

"Well, it's just a real pleasure to meet you folks," says
Rand at the central kiosk. "All I need is proof of
residence, and we'll get this registration party started."

My mother clocks his bushy sideburns, desperate for
a trim, the Kermit the Frog necktie peeking between
buttons of his denim vest. It's all she can do not
to roll her eyes.

"Now will you be living here full-time or just
part of the year?"

"*Part*," she clarifies. "We have a house in Seattle,
symphony tickets, that sort of thing."

He nods, hands the forms to my father.

"And then of course there are the grandkids
in Burlington, so we spend a fair amount of time
in Vermont."

"Well, *that* is quite a coinky-dink!" Rand exclaims, lifting his glasses to the crown of his head, squinting gleefully at both of them.

"You're not going to believe this, but you've got three guesses as to where my people are from!"

THE HUB OF THE UNIVERSE

Guess what? My husband and I are moving
from Burlington, Vermont, to Boston!
Jeffrey was just offered a position teaching at
a prestigious medical school. We're not sure
which one yet—maybe Harvard or MIT or
UMass. Does it really matter? It's prestigious!

But the best news is, Boston is so big everyone
knows something about it, even if they've never
been, even if they've only watched a few episodes
of *Boston Legal* before deciding it's way too liberal.
The city is large and familiar, yet people have
a way of staying anonymous. We're very private
after all. Our landline has always been unlisted.

If we have to move—and we really do—the timing
couldn't be better with the twins starting preschool
in the fall. They're quite accelerated, you know.
I may have said already, but they were toilet-trained
before they could even say a word. It's the British
way, the way I was trained. Now they sight-read
letters, speak simple sentences in English, Spanish,
and French. They can count all the way to fifty
without help.

It's hard to say which suburb we'll choose or
what I'll do with my days once the moving
dust has settled. I'm sure I'll spend some time
browsing local historical sites. (I just love culture!)
I'll take a tour of the Old North Church, buy
us season tickets to the Pops, try a slice of that
famous Boston cream pie (just a small one!),
take up power-walking with new friends
around the well-known Boston Harbor.

We're eager, of course, for my parents
to visit. Jeffrey and my dad love golfing
together, which leaves more time for Mom
and me to browse the Outlets. Some of
the best ones are near the Berkshires, though,
so we might need to take a girl's getaway
weekend. (Fortunately, Jeffrey's mother
can always come down and stay with the kids.)

Did you know Filene's Basement started
in Massachusetts? Did you know there's a
Boston Flower and Garden Show every spring?
Did you know Massachusetts became the first
state to legalize same-sex marriage back in 2004,
the same year *Boston Legal* began?

Across the miles, my mother leans against her
luxury appliances, frowning. She can't
imagine why I'd ruin such a lovely story
by bringing up a thing like that.

BOSTON MARRIAGE

Even if we had met in Boston instead of Bellingham;
even if you had not been wearing your green sweater
with the wool sash askew, or driving your Mercury
Tracer with Tennessee plates, David Gray blasting
from the Discman you had rigged to your radio—
I know I would have loved you: then as now, there
as anywhere.

Even if I had not been wearing my high-water
pants with red sneakers and dark woven belt
(what a catch I was!), or that Rhoda Morgenstern
throw-back scarf in my still-permed hair; even if
we had not been twenty-two and twenty-three,
respectively, you brand-new to the West Coast
and me never having left it once before—
I know I would have loved you: then as now,
there as anywhere.

Even if we were two women older and otherwise
occupied, enlightened enough to recognize a sudden
flutter in the gut is not admissible as empirical evidence,
I can picture it: my son at the pre-pre-school program
for exceptional suburban achievers, my daughter

at the Tchaikovsky and Tots summer music camp;
me, other side of town, following my GPS to the closest
Whole Foods because I didn't have time to bake
the gluten-free birthday cake I promised.
(My husband's colleague's wife has Celiac's, poor
dear, and I'm in charge of preparations for her party!)

Perhaps you're late for a meeting. Perhaps you
just popped in for a hummus wrap with sprouts
and a nice strong coffee. Perhaps I dent your Volvo
hatchback in the parking lot with my monstrous
minivan, the one we're planning to upgrade
to a Mercedes station wagon. It's no secret, I've
been distracted since the move, and I'm hoping
if I wait right here beside your sporty two-door and
apologize profusely and write you a check that you'll
consider not reporting me to my unforgiving insurance
company. (The fact is, there have been a few other
incidents, and I don't want our rates to spike again
just because "Babylon" came on, and I was singing
along with the sun in my eyes...)

And this I can see clearly: you walking toward me
through a checkerboard of silver Audis and black
Saabs; the late-thirties librarian version of you,
which is much like the early-twenties graduate student

version, just more resplendent; still with your long stride and your tousled hair and that furtive look you have been known to wear, appraising me first with well-earned suspicion—*Who is this soccer mom loitering beside your car? Is she actually leaning against your door?*—but soon something between us will shift. We'll have to exchange phone numbers so I can get the damage fixed. And then we'll be waiting outside the body shop, which is already charged with metaphor, and we'll decide to get some lunch at the corner café, where one thing will lead, tenuously at first, then undeniably toward another.

"Not if you hit my car!" Real You insists in the dim glow of our real-life living room. Real You thinks I'm a hopeless romantic, can't be trusted with such a wild subjunctive, since I have a weakness for movies like *Serendipity* ("Absolute shit!" you say, which is true— I won't dispute), but also *Sliding Doors,* which even you admit was charming. See how they end up together anyway, sooner or later, the two who are meant to be?

"They're not even gay," Real You grumbles. It's true, we need more queerly beloveds, don't we? Oh, the puns I am capable of! I place my real hand in your real hand, tell you again how I would have loved you: then as now, there as anywhere. And the real gift is that you believe me.

INTERMISSION AT BENAROYA HALL

In the ladies' room, my mother teases her
hair with a bright blue Pic, then blots the
coral from her lips and applies a fresh coat.
In the mirror behind her, a floral tunic
and a poodle-dog bob are coming,
ever so slowly, into view.

"Linda? Is that you?" Then, a doughy
hand drops, decisive, on her shoulder.

"Bernice?"

"Yes! It's me!" She draws my mother
to her bosom for an awkward hug before
guiding them both toward one of the
vacant divans.

"It's been *ages*! I haven't seen you in any
of the usual places for—well—it must be
going on a decade now!"

"Has it really been that long?"

My mother struggles to keep her knees
from clacking. She squeezes them tight
by crossing her legs, which she has always
resented for being too large—not tapered
like the candle-stick limbs she admires.

"Yes, yes—*at least*! I was beginning to think
something was wrong, but then I ran into
Mabel Huntington, and she told me your
husband had retired and that you're
traveling more these days."

Now my mother relaxes, just a smidge.
Maybe Bernice hasn't heard any of the ugly
rumors after all.

"Well, yes—as a matter of fact, we are.
And, as you may know, our daughter got married."

"Oh, *married*? I did hear she had found someone.
Well, that's lovely, isn't it?" Bernice shows all her
teeth when she smiles and most of her gums.
"She's had some other successes, too, hasn't she,
your Julie?"

The lights dim for a moment, and the first bells begin to ring. To my mother, they must sound like angels singing.

"*Two* of them!" she exclaims, opening her billfold so the pictures of the twins cascade like a plastic waterfall.

"Oh, my! I hadn't realized! Congratulations." Bernice looks down at her hands, hesitates before asking: "Did she carry the twins herself, or perhaps—the other one did?"

My mother, nearly composed again, has the sudden sensation of sinking, or shrinking—she isn't sure which, or if it matters. "The other one?"

"Oh—what would you call her? I'm not very good at these things." Bernice's hand on my mother's wrist burns like a freshly struck match. "The other *mother*, I suppose?"

Now she can't be sure if the bells have rung again or not. Her ears seem to be filling with water, the way they did that summer as a child, the year she nearly drowned.

"I'm afraid I'm not following you, Bernice."

"Well, it's just that—here." Bernice reaches inside her brocade clutch and withdraws a phone. "I know, I know," she laughs. "The grandkids thought I needed one, and as it turns out, I just love this little Android! It goes with everything and makes me feel downright *god-like*! Now give me a minute—"

"Ladies, intermission is about to end," an attendant calls from the door.

My mother stands, then sways, then seats herself again to keep from toppling.

The long pink nails are tapping like the beaks of tiny birds. "Isn't this Julie?" Bernice asks, pointing to a picture of me at the Lambda Literary Awards in New York City.

"She looks very pretty—quite feminine, all in all— but she's being honored for having written something—" Bernice's voice dips dramatically now—"*Sapphic.*"

My mother is sinking, that much she knows, vision fading. With her last audible breath, she spits out the words: "That's not her."

"But it says in the caption—"

Then my mother, not quite like Jesus, though he does
come to her mind, begins unexpectedly to rise:

"There are *plenty* of young women who have her name,
Bernice. Why, they must have turned out *dozens* of Julie
Marie Wades in 1979! Her library books were always
getting mixed up with another girl's, right in our own
neighborhood!" (This is true.) "And one is a Starbuck's
executive today, always donating money and doing that
Race for the Cure!" (This is true also.)

Linda Wade plants her heels deep
in the plush carpet, lets indignation
do the heavy lifting. "*My* Julie isn't even
Julie *Wade* anymore! She's married,
to a surgeon, and they're living in Boston
now! She took *his* name, of course,
because that's the kind of daughter we raised!"

Soon, my mother is running into the dim light
like diving into a swimming pool at dusk.
Lucky for her, my father glows in the dark.
He stands alone in the lobby like a trench-

coated isotope. He knows better than
to ask questions.

My father drives her home before the second act,
the only time they've ever left a show midway.
All the while, behind her, Bernice had been calling out:
"Okay, okay, but it's not so bad, is it really? I mean,
even our former Vice President's daughter is gay!"
And then: "It doesn't mean she's a *Democrat*, Linda!"
(This we should leave for another day.)

MARY CHENEY, YOU KNOW WHAT THEY SAY ABOUT WOMEN LIKE US

That we're dykes because we have daddy issues.

That we're queer because we aligned ourselves with the wrong parent early on, then grew a fondness for wide pant legs and flat-heeled shoes.

That we're bitter because nobody asked us to Prom.

Listen, this isn't me talking. I'm just trying to keep up with the pseudo-science.

We might be lesbians because our mothers withheld their approval all our lives, or perhaps because they never showed us how to mold the meatballs right.

Your mother told Cokie Roberts on national TV, "Mary has never declared such a thing!" At the time, you had been out and living with your partner for eight years.

Maybe we watched too few episodes of *Father Knows Best* and/or didn't identify enough with Jane Wyatt.

Mother Knows Less? Mother Keeps Quiet? Mother Makes Him Think It Was All His Idea?

In 2000, your father said, "I think we ought to do everything we can to tolerate and accommodate whatever kind of relationships people want to enter into."

Gee, Dick, thanks for that rousing endorsement. I'm glad you can tolerate and accommodate the generous stick up your ass, all while still supporting the Federal Marriage Amendment.

Forgive me, Mary. He's your dad. If it helps, my father called him "a real swell guy." And besides, my dad never said anything about tolerance *or* accommodation. Instead:

"This whole homosexuality business started in the 1960s. Your mother and I got married, then watched the world around us fall to the fornicators and the bigamists and the sodomites."

Note how he doesn't see a correlation there—that maybe *their* marriage tipped the iceberg toward some more promising alternatives.

In 2004, you said you came "very close" to quitting your job on the Bush-Cheney re-election campaign. People were wearing buttons at the RNC that read, *One man. One woman. As God intended.* Chanting it, too. Forget about quitting your job; I don't see how you didn't quit your party.

Or maybe it's me who's lacking patience, compassion, the long-sightedness to see things through. Maybe I should stand in awe of such restraint, the fact you never seem to find the last straw in the haystack of shit they heap upon you.

The pay-off? You and Heather are still invited to spend Christmas in Jackson Hole. Meanwhile, I couldn't find my parents' second home on a map, and they have never once uttered my partner's name.

In your autobiography, you quote yourself as saying: "Personally, I'd rather not be known as the vice-president's lesbian daughter." Why not? Is it too reductive, too making-an-issue-out-of-a-person? See, I thought Republicans always liked that.

I'm not fond of epithets or bald-face denials, but I'd really get my back up if anyone presumed such a thing about me—*Republican*? Because my parents are? This apple fell so far from that blazing red tree she has rolled into another garden.

Lesbians love turquoise, I hear. Sapphire is my birthstone. Cerulean the color of my aura, a psychic once said. *Lavender menace*? That's fine in theory, but Mary Cheney, come with me. Wouldn't you like to menace in blue?

DREAM JOURNAL, BOSTON SUBURBS

I begin to speculate about the something wrong
between us. It's his long hours at the hospital
perhaps, in the classroom, on the lecture circuit
year after year. I miss him. Surely I do. I miss
sailing together on the Chesapeake, ice-skating
at Rockefeller Center, candlelight and lobster tail
at that little place we love in Kennebunk, so close
to where the Bushes live.

And after all, no woman is a grand marble island
in a gourmet kitchen, entire of herself.
Every woman is a part of the cornice, the valence,
one shelf of the teak bookcase built into the wall.

I consult the ladies' magazines to be sure of how
I feel. The pictures unfailingly confirm.
What woman doesn't long to sip Pinot Grigio
and peck at crudité while the man of her dreams
dines beside her on frites and filet she has prepared?

Consider also the fine sinew of his forearms, rolled
sleeves of the white Oxford shirt, collar loosened
and tie cast back over his sculpted shoulder—

a courtesy to *her*—so no spill will blemish
the impeccable fabric she once chose.

But dreams are a dead giveaway, aren't they, and
where are the men in mine? While my mother wrote
the story of my waking life, I was dreaming all those
years of Jodie Foster in *Silence of the Lambs*, Elizabeth
Montgomery on *Bewitched*. Mrs. Miller, my fourth-grade
teacher, slipped under my eyelids every night,
the way hallway light slips, nearly unnoticed,
under a bedroom door.

By college, the pert young women in purple jerseys
with lean muscles in their legs, ponytails pulled through
baseball caps, clean short nails, held me rapt for hours
as I slept. Which is another way of saying: I would have
gladly walked cleat-less through the damp, mud-luscious
grass, dragging their water coolers and their mesh bags
of lacrosse sticks and catchers' mitts behind me.

Oh, how I wanted to caddy for them, to be their
referee or their umpire or someone, *anyone*,
authorized to stand in close proximity without
arousing suspicion on those fields.

I hadn't yet realized that I could join their team,
pull the same purple jersey over my head, the same
tall socks up to my knees. Which is another way
of saying: I hadn't yet dreamed that one day
one of those girls might dream of me.

SHOOTING POOL WITH
ANNE HECHE THE DAY AFTER
ELLEN AND PORTIA'S WEDDING

For starters, the waiter was slow as fuck
bringing our beers, and Heche kept
punching her tiny fist against her pink
splayed palm and muttering,
"Somebody's about to get clobbered."

"Aw, you're just sore…" I say, trailing off,
thinking about the backroom broadcast and
the white-on-white cover of *People* magazine.

Now she's snapping her gum and strutting
around this green velvet like she owns the place,
and I'm starting to feel that itch in my throat
that means both intrigue and fear.

"Go ahead," she says. "Tell me something *terrible*
about myself."

I could tell her how we call it "getting heched"
when a woman you like, or love, leaves you
for a man. I could explain that, unlike the tired

Uhaul jokes, she's still with us, fresh as a paper
cut that starts small, then seems to gnaw and gnaw.

But when I look at her, quick appraisal under
the low-hanging light—her tight pale arms,
her compact body beneath the red ribbed tank
top and cut-off shorts—it's a feeling like not-quite-
attraction and not-quite-compassion.
I play it off with a wave:

I say, "Don't you know by now you're America's
favorite hasbian?" Yeah, I thought she'd like that.
Heche takes a bow. Her taut green veins stand out
everywhere in stunning ovation. The adrenaline
glides from her hand to the cue on a luge of newly
polished intention.

"Goddamn right I am!" she grins. "Now watch me put
this ball in that pocket."

WHAT DATE RAPE AND
GAY MARRIAGE HAVE IN COMMON

It's the making something smaller, see. Shrinking it,
paring it down. It's the less-than symbol disguised
as simple adjective, trying to upgrade from coach to
compound noun: Date Rape < Rape. Gay Marriage
< Marriage.

<

It's the Pinocchio Complex, see. Not quite as real
as *Rape*, not quite as real as *Marriage.* Synthetic
somehow, highly sanitized: surely not flesh and
blood, not here and now. Surely not a real-life boy-
and-girl, (boy-and-boy, (girl-and-girl…doing God
knows what to each other.

It can happen so many ways, *for better or worse, for
richer or poorer*…All these possible permutations
are likely to trip us up. We need our rapists in back
woods and dark alleys, stocking-capped strangers
rising out of the fog. We need our weddings in
churches, a 1:1 ratio of skirts to suits, bouquets to
boutonnieres. We need to know the thing we know
isn't really something else, so we call it less-than, see.

<

Do you remember what our math teachers said
about the way the parted lips should face? The
smaller opening toward the larger, toward the thing
of greater weight? Mine said to think of it like Pac-
Man eating pac-dots, which are small blips inside a
blue maze, easy enough to consume.

So the mouth is always eating that which comes
after it, making it less than it was before. The way
date is taking a bite out of rape, taking a bite out of
crime. (Take that, McGruff. The way some marriages
are whittled down like old wood—valid Here-But-
Not-There, There-But-Not-Here. (Mythical, in some
places, as Atlantis.

Date Rape < Rape. Gay Marriage < Marriage.

<

But what will we tell the school kids, the
fraternities, the county clerks, the beer distributors?
What reparations will be made to Vera Wang and
Jose Cuervo? Will there be white space on the docket
or the Christmas card?

Think of the things we'll have to think of that we never thought before. Like when the "stewardess" became a "flight attendant" and stopped wearing her jaunty hat. Order a Clamato juice and sip on that for a while. Does it take you back? Think of all the parentheses we'll never remember to close.

))))

THE SURGEON IN NEW ENGLAND, ALTERNATE ENDING #1

Sometimes I wait for my husband
beneath the wisteria arbor in our front yard.
He parks his Lexus on the circular drive,
scratches his five o' clock shadow—
though it is well past ten—then asks me
if I had any trouble putting the children
to bed. I didn't. It's strange how I hardly
ever think of them. Dinner is warming
in the oven: rosemary lamb with fingerling
potatoes. Where I learned to cook this way,
I'll never know.

Tonight I say, "Jeffrey, we need to talk."
The wrap around my shoulders, for there
is a light chill, has a special name. It's called
a pashmina. My in-laws have given me one
in almost every color. When I search my
drawers, I cannot find so much as a
sweatshirt anymore.

"Uh-oh." Jeffrey makes a sad puppy face,
the same one he offers his patients when

he's kept them waiting too long wearing
only a flimsy gown. "Did I miss Date Night?
I know you told me we were going to sync
our Apple calendars, but—"

"I'd like a divorce," Pashmina-Me murmurs
with her finest, flattest affect.

My husband thinks I'm being dramatic,
of course. "A divorce—over Date Night?
That hardly solves the problem, does it?"

He sits beside me now on the wrought-iron
bench, swivels the platinum band on the fourth
finger of his left hand. "Julie, my love, tell me
how I can make this up to you."

"You seem like a very nice man." I pat
his knee as though he were a child.
Perhaps my maternal instinct is emerging after
all? "In so many years together, it's a shame
we didn't get to know each other better.
It wasn't possible, I realize, but still."

"So, you're serious?" He's loosening his tie,
the one I bought for him last year: burgundy

with little flecks of gold, a just-because gift,
Pierre Cardin.

"Almost always, in this narrative."

We both shiver a little now, wonder if we
should go inside. "But the good news is:
a single doctor with sole custody of
two presumably perfect kids—you can
skip right from one-night stand to second
wife if you like." I smile at him,
my first real smile.

"What do *you* like?" He sits holding his tie
in hand, defeated but stoic. No one has ever
scripted him tears.

"That's a question people never ask you
when they're afraid to hear the answer."

"Should I be afraid?" He lifts his eyes.
"I honestly can't tell."

"Don't worry," I say, rising to my feet
in the pumps that pinch my toes.
I'm dropping these at the first Goodwill

I pass. "Fear around here is like hiccups,
Dear: short-lived and soon enough forgotten."

Jeffrey remains calm. He's surprised, possibly
even stricken, but there's always been
something unflappable about him.
He cuts into hearts with a steady hand,
listens to ragtime as he stanches blood.

"Will you write to me?" the surgeon
in New England asks.

"It's unlikely, Jeff," I say, tugging my slim
luggage case onto the soapstone path.
My flight to Fort Lauderdale departs
in just two hours.

"But I promise that I will write *about* you."

IN PERPETUITY, I SHALL REMAIN THE QUESTION MY PARENTS GUESS WRONG ON *JEOPARDY!*

Bellingham, Washington; February 24, 2014

There is snow on the road, which some might consider an omen. Not us. Not after two years of Florida swelter, of longing to be colder, of liking at least a *suggestion* of winter. Ice on the windowsills. Frost on the grass. A shiver sharp as good luck.

We wear black dresses. Not so fancy we couldn't wear them again—though we haven't. We carry bright flowers from the Farmer's Market, arranged by your sister into bouquets we won't toss until the next day—and then, only over our shoulders, only into the Bay.

How strange it was to write where our parents were born in order to procure the license—to have to print their names on that form at all. A narrative altered but never erased. A lineage notarized into law by one county clerk or another. No true new beginnings. And what if we lied or didn't know or

refused to remember—would we be denied our right
to wed, again?

But here is the sun recusing itself from the day, and
here the upper room of Le Chat Noir, flooded with
errant light. Here are eleven friends assembled—one
officiating, one reading a poem, another signing
as witness to the speaking of vows, the sharing of
rings, and two little girls playing pretend-wedding
afterwards while no one rushes in to say what our
mothers always said—*girls can't marry other girls!*
They said this often, with words and without them,
the complex machinery of their speech and silence,
the fields they plowed deep in us, so the dream of
this day was impossibly furrowed. Our fathers, who
denied such dreams could exist.

We do not smash cake into each other's mouths or
toss garters to a flock of eager groomsmen. There are
no groomsmen, and no bridesmaids either, which
means no one is singled out for being single or
dubbed a "matron" because she has already signed
on a dotted line, given herself to another.

I am not thinking of my parents' house two hours
south of here, or of their other house at the shore,

the one I have never seen. I am not thinking of the weathervane on their roof that announces THE WADES live here, or of the elephantine hedges that swell along their borders, in order to mask the fence that masks the yard. The contradiction in terms: declaring themselves, then hiding. I am not even thinking of the difference between secrecy and privacy, which was once explained to me as the difference between what we carry as shame and what we keep for ourselves as an act of self-respect.

I was not ashamed, and yet I cannot believe it was self-respect that compelled me once, from the post office in this very town, to make six photocopies of my thesis—that first collection of lesbian love poems—and then to address six manila envelopes with such meticulous script to the residences of their most cherished friends. "Your mother had to give up her clubs because of you!" my father chided through the phone. "You shamed her in front of everyone!" And though it was my right to claim my love, I regret I ever once used love to punish someone else, even if it was my mother, who could not love the woman I had become.

No, I am not thinking of them as we cross the threshold into our room at The Chrysalis, a grand hotel for which they were breaking ground just as we moved away. But if I were, I would send a small blessing to my parents watching *Jeopardy!* in one of their homes, eating popcorn and drinking Shasta (diet, of course), my mother impassioned as she calls out, "What is Burma, Alex?" and "What is the Prime Meridian?"

I am not thinking of them, though, or how even if they knew I had just married my true love on their side of the country, neither would have found the— *what would you call it, Alex?—the wherewithal?*—to come.

THE GAME OF LIFE

Since our benefits are administered through the Division of State Group Insurance (DSGI) we will have to obtain legislature direction on the approval for benefits for same-sexy [sic] marriages. To date, we have not obtained any guidance supporting this initiative.
> —Correspondence from Human Resources,
> August 27, 2014

Six months since our nuptials,
    and still the law in limbo.
Even my employer resorts
    to cryptic legalese.
"This is how it feels to be
    living in a typo,

where all the world is parsed
    into hetero and homo."
My Outlaws are the choir
    that already agrees.
Six months since our nuptials,
    and still the law in limbo.

Now our niece has stamped her feet
          and stands with arms akimbo:
"Girls are the pink people, boys are
          the blue! Take your pieces, *please!*"
Further confirmation that
          I am living in a typo

where my Pepto-Bismol proxy
          steers me through the shallows
to a square where I win marriage
          like a whopping shopping spree.
Six months since our nuptials,
          and still the law in limbo.

"Pink people marry blue people!"
          Evie squeals in child-argot,
reaching for my blueberry groom
          before her mother intervenes.
This is how it feels to be
          living in a typo:

(Wink) *Cinderella didn't have a pre-nup.*
          (Cough) *Barbie's not a bimbo.*
"Remember when you danced
          at the wedding of your aunties?"

Six months since our nuptials,
        and still the law in limbo.
"Someday," my love assures me,
        "we'll strike through that typo."

THE SURGEON IN NEW ENGLAND, ALTERNATE ENDING #2

We're at the Club, of course. It's the weekend. He's been playing squash with our children's pediatrician, Ted or Tom, says he'll meet me poolside after his steam, after my swim. Somehow we always find each other.

Now I'm drinking pink lemonade and letting my hair dry natural in the sun. I don't mind his lateness. I never did. I'm watching other women glide through the water—breaststroke, backstroke, and butterfly—while at the same time, I'm pretending not to watch.

"Hey, Darling," Jeffrey says, kissing my cheek, slipping into the empty seat beside me. He's wearing a cologne I despise, but otherwise, looks fit and tan, always handsome in his white shorts and lavender polo shirt. Never so much as a stray hair, a gash from shaving.

"What do you think? Is this a good time to talk?"

I shrug. "As good as any, I suppose."

He flags down a server, orders a double scotch.
"This is nice, right?" he sighs. "This life?"

"Sure. Some people seem to relish it."

"What about you? Do you relish it, Julie?"

I try to meet his eyes, but the light is bright, and he's
wearing his transition lenses.

"Jeffrey, why don't you say what's really on your mind?
You might find we have something in common."

Now his drink has arrived—neat, of course. No
reason to dilute anything with ice. He takes a sip,
then takes my hand. "Just say it? Just put it out
there, all my cards on the table?"

I nod and stroke the light hairs on his knuckles
with unexpected tenderness.

"I'm in love with someone else." His jaw snaps.
"Do you hate me?"

No, just your cologne. This isn't what I say,
of course. Jeffrey sips more scotch, and I more

lemonade, and in the slow, unfolding silence,
I feel as though I can finally breathe.

"Is it Ted?" I ask.

He looks up. "Do you mean Tom?"

"Yes. *Tom*. I mean Tom. Are you in love
with him?"

Startled at first, then relieved: "How did you
know?"

Now I am free to release my first belly-laugh in years.
I laugh so hard my teeth un-whiten, my brows un-
Botox, my nails un-manicure and de-gloss. I begin
to resemble myself again.

"Would it be terribly insensitive to you in your
big coming-out moment if I said, *Takes one to
know one?*"

"You? What? No!" Jeffrey regards me with sudden
admiration. When I finally stop laughing, he leans
over and clinks my glass. "I'm impressed."

"Really?"

"Well, you fooled me for fourteen years!"

"But is that saying so much?"

For the first time in our married life, he guffaws.
"OK then. Touché."

Jeffrey settles again, takes my hand as more
than a gesture this time. "So—are you in love
with someone, too? Is that a naïve question?"

"Of course," I say. "Anything less would be
a waste of time."

He cocks his head, and I continue. "It's a line from a
poem I love, a poem I read years ago just before I met
the woman I've been carrying this faithful torch for."

We order another round of drinks and then another.
I pull a pair of Old Navy flip-flops out of my bag. See
how my feet spontaneously un-pumice, how the fancy
highlights disappear from my no-longer-salon-quality hair.

"You been carrying those around for fourteen years,
too?" He nudges me, and I nudge him back. We have
an inside joke now. We are old friends at last.

"Look at you two!" Lonnie Milford pauses at
our table. I notice her Coach bag, her sandals
with heels, her gold sarong. I recall her long history
flirting with my husband

"I just stopped by to say hello, and—" hand to clavicle—
"I must admit, I feel like I'm interrupting something!"

Jeffrey waves his glass in the air. "That's because you are!"

"Oh, you're bad!" I whisper, though I'm giggling, too.
"We have to stop this. People are staring."

"Honey, I'm just getting started!"

We agree to go home. We agree to tell each other
everything over nachos with Rotel dip and RC Cola.
No one is going to cook or do the dishes. We have a
microwave. We have a can opener. We can put our feet
on the furniture for a change.

"I want to marry Tom," Jeff grins at me. "The goddamn
Supreme Court of the United States says I can, and *fuck*
anyone who tries to stop us!"

He's a little drunk, so I take the keys
and guide him toward the car.
"Fuck 'em," I nod.

As I buckle him into the front seat, I touch
the perfect part in his hair, marvel at the massive
quantity of pomade he must require. He's about
to nod off, I think, but all at once, Jeffrey seizes
my wrist, and his lenses transition back to clear.

"Oh. My. God. I just thought of something. Can you
imagine what your mother is going to say?" I chuckle
and touch his cheek, peer into those deep blue eyes
she gave him. "I'm serious, Julie! It's bad enough
with *you* being gay, but *me*—the perfect son-in-law?
Doctor Do-No-Wrong?"

"I think it's very healthy that you refer to yourself
that way."

"Not *me*! Your *mother*! That woman's a real piece
of work, you know." I know.

"I mean, your dad probably thinks you can pray
the gay away, but what in the hell is your mother
going to do?"

Now the engine roars to life at my command.
I smile and kiss the hand of my sweet, subjunctive
husband. "Don't worry about her, Jeff.
I have a hunch she'll think of something."

ACKNOWLEDGMENTS

No poet is an island, entire of herself. These are my bridges, my rowboats, my life preservers:

I am grateful to and for all the writers and teachers who have guided me toward my own good life of writing and teaching, including Jani Miller, Kathe Curran, Sister Rosemary Perisich, Carolyn Du Pen, Sister Janice Holkup, Sally McLaughlin, David Seal, Suzanne Paola, Bruce Beasley, Brenda Miller, Steve VanderStaay, Kathryn Flannery, Lisa Parker, Lucy Fischer, Tracy K. Smith, Toi Derricotte, Annette Allen, Cate Fosl, and Paul Griner.

I cherish especially the extraordinary and ongoing mentorship of Tom Campbell and Dana Anderson.

My colleagues and students in the Creative Writing program at Florida International University are never less than inspiring. Thank you especially to Lynne Barrett, Térèse Campbell, Cindy Chinelly, Debra Dean, John Dufresne, Denise Duhamel, Marta Lee, Campbell McGrath, and Les Standiford for reminding me every day why this is my dream job.

I cannot fully convey my gratitude to Lawrence
Schimel at A Midsummer Night's Press for his
investment in and relentless support of my work, yet
here, once again, I try.

I am also honored by the generous blurbs offered by
Oliver de la Paz, Aaron Smith, and Stacey Waite.

"The Game of Life" is dedicated to my poetry heroes,
Denise Duhamel and Maureen Seaton, who helped
me believe in my own latent, neo-formalist powers.
This poem is my first villanelle and is written under
their shimmering influence.

Always, I thank the friends who have loved me best
and longest—Anna Rhodes and James Allen Hall.

Always, I thank the Outlaws, who acknowledged me
as family years before the Law did—Kim, Matt, Evie,
Nolan "Super Hondo," and now Sam Striegel!

Always, and most of all, I thank my favorite person,
Angie Griffin, for the great adventure of our fifteen
years together and for these past four years of same-
sexy marriage.

•••

This collection exists, in one sense, because a half century ago a salesman named William Wade and a schoolteacher named Linda Smith began their married life with a ceremony at Phinney Ridge Lutheran Church in Seattle, Washington. Twelve years later, they began to raise their only child together. As I hope this book reflects, despite many divergences from the expected path, I have learned great devotion from my father, fierce resilience and strong imagination from my mother. I am forged, in the end, by their two incomparable fires.

In another sense, this collection exists because John Dufresne, my friend, mentor, and frequent companion in the peripatetic method, encouraged me to write a novel based on the strange daughter-doppelgänger my mother had conjured—that heterosexual doctor's wife I did not in fact become. Who knows? Maybe I'll write a novel next time. For now, Johnny D., one of the finest people and storytellers I know, this novella in poems is for you.

•••

The epigraph to this collection comes from the poem "Love" by Tom Crawford, which appears in the June 1999 issue of *Willow Springs*.

The poem "Shooting Pool with Anne Heche the Day Before Ellen and Portia's Wedding" appears in the Spring 2010 issue of *Dislocate*.

The poem "What Date Rape and Gay Marriage Have in Common" appears in the Spring/Summer 2016 issue of *PANK*.

The poems "Intermission at Benaroya Hall," "Dream Journal, Boston Suburbs," "The Game of Life," and "The Surgeon in New England, Alternate Ending #1" appear in the 2018 issue of *Cherry Tree*.

The poem "In Perpetuity, I Shall Remain the Question My Parents Guess Wrong on *Jeopardy!*" was featured in the SWWIM (Supporting Women Writers in Miami) Poem-A-Day Series on October 25, 2017. It is a 2017 nominee for the Pushcart Prize.

The poems "Boston Marriage" and "Mary Cheney, You Know What They Say About Women Like Us" appear in the Summer 2018 issue of *Southern Women's Review*, guest-edited by Ashley M. Jones